67 MORNING RITUAL HABITS FOR YOUR BODY, MIND & SPIRIT

Stefan James

TABLE OF CONTENTS

INTRODUCTION 1

BODY 5

Water 6

Go For A Walk 6

Stretch 9

Do Yoga 10

Use A Foam Roller 10

Lift Weights 11

Cardiovascular Exercise 12

Practice Deep Breathing 13

Use PEMF Therapy 14

Do A Salt Water Flush 16

Brush Teeth & Floss 17

Use A Neti Pot 17

Take A Cold Shower 19

Take Supplements 19

Enjoy Red Light Therapy 21

Scrape Your Tongue 22

Practice Oil Pulling 23

Juicing 24

Practice Rebounding 26

Dry Brush Your Skin   27

Drink A Smoothie   28

Dancing   29

Coffee Enemas   30

Laughing   31

Take A Wheatgrass Shot   32

Practice Wim Hof's Breathing Technique   34

Drink Something Green   35

Weigh Yourself   35

Use A Sun Light Therapy Light   36

MIND   38

Recite Affirmations   39

Meditation   40

Reading   41

Recite Your Mission Statement   42

Practice Gratitude   43

Ask Yourself Empowering Questions   44

Listen To An Audiobook Or Podcast   46

Watch An Inspiring Video   47

Listen to Binaural Beats   49

Write and Read Out Goals   50

Create A Vision Board   51

Find An Accountability Buddy   52

Visualization   54

Plan Out Your Day   55

Make Your Bed   57

Focus On Your Highest Leverage Activity   58

Reading Quotes   59

Listen to Uplifting Music   60

Read Your Life Vision Out Loud   61

Journaling   62

Emotional Flood   63

Use NLP To Anchor Emotional States   66

Reflect On Your Life Values And What's Most Important
To You   68

SPIRIT   70

Express Gratitude   71

Practice Forgiveness   72

Random Acts of Kindness   74

Guided Meditation   75

Ho'oponopono Prayer   77

Prayer   78

Heart Meditation   79

Celebrate You   80

Self-Love   81

Recite A Mantra   83

Set An Intention For The Day   84

Write A Love Letter To Yourself   85

Record Your Dreams   86

Practice Your Spirituality   87

Read Spiritual Text   89

NEXT STEPS   90

INTRODUCTION

Dear Friend,

When I was 17 years old, I discovered that the most successful and happiest people in the world all have morning rituals.

Successful people aren't successful by chance or luck. There are consistent things they're doing every single morning and throughout their day, that set them up to win. They have certain habits, beliefs, behaviors, and ways of thinking.

Bill Gates starts his mornings on the treadmill, while simultaneously feeding his mind via watching courses from the Teaching Company.

Benjamin Franklin used to wake up at 4:00 am, and proactively think about what he wanted to accomplish for the day. He would ask himself the question, "What good shall I do this day?"

Steve Jobs spent his mornings re-evaluating his work and desires. In his speech to a graduating class at Stanford, Jobs said, "For the past 33 years I have looked in the mirror every morning and asked myself: 'If today were the last day of my life, would I want to do what I am about to do today?' And whenever the answer has been 'No' for too many days in a row, I know I need to change something.

Oprah Winfrey's morning ritual consists of clearing her mind with at least 20 minutes of meditation. Oprah says about after her morning ritual: "I walked away feeling fuller than when I'd come in. Full of hope, a sense of contentment, and deep joy. Knowing for sure that even in the daily craziness that bombards us from every direction, there is — still — the constancy of stillness. Only from that space can you create your best work and your best life."

Tony Robbins has an elaborate one-hour morning ritual he calls the "Hour of Power". He claims that a major element of his sustained energy and focus comes from his intense and unusual morning ritual.

If you study the most successful and happiest people throughout history, you'll find that they all have one important habit in common: an empowering morning ritual.

How about the average person?

Unfortunately, the average person wakes up reactive, rather than being proactive about their day.

They hear the alarm, and then immediately slam the snooze button to get in a few extra minutes of sleep.

When they finally do wake up, they feel tired, exhausted, and unmotivated. They're flooded with stress and anxiety about all of the things they have to do that day, which is often why people resort to frantically checking their e-mail or scrolling through social media as a way to escape and get temporary gratification.

They make a cup of coffee just so that they can function and make it through the day.

Then they eat a quick, unhealthy breakfast and rush out the door for work.

Being proactive instead, and having an empowering morning ritual, has the power to dramatically change every area of your life — including your productivity, happiness, body, fulfillment, health, wealth, spirit, everything.

Having a morning ritual has allowed me to become a multi-millionaire; enjoy excellent health, energy and vitality; attract the woman of my dreams; and most importantly, to feel alive and fulfilled.

I've found that the most effective and empowering morning rituals include at least one ritual for these core areas which I'll guide you through in this book:

Your mind, body, and spirit.

For example, to stimulate and condition your mind every morning you could read inspiring books, condition certain beliefs, condition emotional states, or plan your day.

For your body, you could go for a run, meditate, or do yoga.

To nurture your spirit, you could write down what you're grateful for, contribute in some way to the lives of others, or practice your spiritual beliefs.

There's a lot that you can do, some of which you're likely already aware of, and others you've probably never heard of or thought about before.

I created these life-changing morning ritual habits to help you quickly get ideas for your own morning ritual, and I've categorized them into the three areas: BODY, MIND, and SPIRIT.

Keep in mind, these 67 morning ritual habits are some of my personal favorites, but they aren't the be-all and end-all. No one person is the same and we're all at different stages in our lives. So be flexible with your rituals and try different things!

I wrote this book to provide you with a menu of options in a straightforward manner and without much fluff.

There's a lot of rituals in this book, but understand there is no way you need to or can do ALL of them. Instead, I recommend to try a few of them out and construct your own empowering morning ritual that empowers you each day.

It's my utmost desire to inspire you to cultivate the consistent habit of a morning ritual in your life.

If you commit to a morning ritual every day for then next 30 days, whether it's for 15 minutes, 30 minutes, 60 minutes or longer - I have no doubt you'll see the incredible benefits of it and will stick with it for the rest of your life.

Here's to living a life of energy, fulfillment and abundance.

Sincerely,

Stefan James

Founder of Project Life Mastery
www.projectlifemastery.com

BODY

Your physical body is your temple and is the vehicle that allows us to achieve and experience everything in our lives. If we fail to continuously nurture and optimize our bodies, then it'll begin to limit what we can experience for the day and affect other areas of our lives.

That's why it's important to include some of these habits in your morning first, first thing upon waking. By turning on your body, it'll turn on your mind for the day and influence your emotions.

Below are some of my favorite rituals for your body.

Water

A lot of people wake up in the morning and immediately reach for a cup of coffee in order to wake them up, but this is only serving to further dehydrate the body.

The moment that you wake up in the morning you should drink 16 to 24 ounces of quality, filtered water on an empty stomach. Doing so immediately rehydrates your body after 7-8 hours of sleep.

In addition to rehydration, research shows that drinking water first thing in the morning boosts your metabolism, helps rid the body of toxins, improves your skin, strengthens the immune system, and prevents kidney stones and bladder infections.

Since nearly 70% of our body is comprised of water, it is essential that we stay hydrated. Instead of drinking coffee first thing in the morning, start your day off right, with a drink that has cleansing and healing effects.

I personally use a water ionizer by Enagic, which helps to filter and increases the antioxidant production potential of the water. You can learn more about Enagic here: http://projectlifemastery.com/enagic

Go For A Walk

Starting your day with a walk in nature is a great moving meditation. It's an opportunity to take some time to reflect, gain appreciation for your surroundings, calm your mind, and collect your thoughts for the day ahead.

Because walking is a low-difficult activity, it allows you to direct your thinking internally to things that matter most to you, which supports a positive mindset. Not only that, but taking this time allows you to 'walk through your day', so to speak, and plan out what you need to accomplish.

Research shows that if you want to add seven years to your lifespan, set aside 20 to 25 minutes for a daily walk. The simple act of walking has been found to trigger an anti-aging process and even help repair old DNA.

It's easy to stumble out of bed and rush to work. Take a few moments to breathe in the fresh air, move your arms, and get your heart pumping Studies show that by consistently walking in the morning at a brisk pace, between 5-6 km per hour, we can reduce our chances of suffering from heart disease by as much as 40%.

Even a little bit of movement can make a massive difference in your physical, mental, and emotional health. In the words of Henry David Thoreau, *"An early morning walk is a blessing for the whole day."*

To enhance your morning walk, try combining it with Breathwalking.

Breathwalking is the science of combining specific patterns of breathing, synchronized with your walking steps, and enhanced with the art of directed, meditative attention.

Breathing and walking are instinctual to many of us, however there is a way to do it correctly.

Many of us are so rushed to get from point A to point B that we forget about the journey in between. Life isn't about "getting" to a certain place. Rather, it's about learning how to enjoy the discovery.

Breathwalking offers many benefits, some of which include decreased anxiety, reduced back pain, and weight loss.

Breathwalking involves bringing your focus inward, quieting the mind, and moving in a more mindful and loving way.

The trick to breathwalking is to coordinate your breathing so that you inhale with four steps, and then exhale with four steps.

Take 10 minutes every morning and walk your way into a more calm and blissful state of mind. When we are consciously aware of how we breathe while walking, we are able to find more joy in each step.

One of my favorite quotes by Thich Nhat Hanh is, *"Walk as if you are kissing the Earth with your feet."*

To learn more about Breathwalking, I recommend the book Breathwalk: Breathing Your Way To A Revitalized Body, Mind an Spirit by Gurucharan Singh Khalsa and Yogi Bhajan.

Stretch

When you wake up in the morning it is natural to experience body stiffness, which is why it is so important to stretch your muscles. As we get older, our flexibility weakens.

The world of technology has created a sedentary culture, which has taken a toll on our bodies, both physically and mentally. Such a simple ritual may seem pointless, but the health benefits of stretching are far-reaching.

Research shows that stretching can improve your posture, eliminate aches and pains in your muscles and joints, increase blood flow to your brain, reduce stress, and promote greater amounts of energy so that you can master your day.

Instead of jumping out of bed, wake your body up gently and give your spine, muscles and joints the love that they deserve. In the words of Bob Anderson, *"If you stretch properly, you will find that every movement that you make becomes easier."*

Do Yoga

There is no better way to calm your mind, set a positive intention, and cleanse your body in the morning than by doing a yoga practice.

As a moving meditation, yoga is a vehicle for self-love and self-discovery. It is a way for you to explore and better understand the connection between your body and mind.

When people talk about yoga, they tend to make reference to the physiological benefits, which include increased flexibility, improved respiration, a balanced metabolism, and weight reduction. However, the real magic of yoga lies in the mental and psychological benefits it provides, which include a reduction in anxiety, depression, and stress, and an improvement in brain functioning.

Whatever you are looking for, yoga has it all. As Sri Sri Ravi Shankar puts it, *"Health is not a mere absence of disease. It is a dynamic expression of life – in terms of how joyful, loving and enthusiastic you are."*

When you commit to making yoga a part of your daily ritual, it can provide a sense of purpose, meaning, and stability in your life.

Use A Foam Roller

In today's digital world, a lot more people are experiencing upper back, shoulder and neck stiffness because they are living sedentary lifestyles. While doing yoga and stretching is great, I encourage you to take it one step further and start using a foam roller.

Referred to as self-myofascial release, using a foam roller is likened to giving your spine a deep tissue massage. Research shows that the foam roller improves athletic performance and flexibility, reduces workout-related soreness, slash recovery time and knocks out muscle pain. As a result, it has become a popular exercise amongst athletes.

By feeling your muscle trigger points with the roller, you can then apply pressure in the exact locations of your body where you are experiencing pain. I encourage you to use a foam roller before and after a workout. Doing so will decrease your risk of injury and increase your recovery time. Are you ready to start rolling?

Lift Weights

Early morning weight training is a great way to start your day. It provides you with a sense of accomplishment, which is a great way to prime your mind for success.

Not only are you strengthening your muscles, but you are also conditioning your mind.

When it comes to goal-setting, there are few feats more challenging than staying committed to a healthy lifestyle. There are so many health benefits to lifting weights, some of which include improved bone density; increased strength of connective tissue, muscles, and tendons; improved sleep; and extended lifespan.

Once you begin to notice the positive physical changes in your body, your mindset will improve as well. With consistent effort, one's willpower can be strengthened, just like any muscle in the body. As the saying goes, *"The pain you feel today will be the strength that you need tomorrow."* Start pumping some iron!

Cardiovascular Exercise

A lot of people have no idea how good their body is designed to feel. Starting your day with a sweaty cardio workout before breakfast is a great way to wake up, get moving, and activate your metabolism.

You don't need to purchase an expensive gym membership in order to stay in shape. You can do things like jumping jacks, burpees, squats, stair climbers, and plank poses, in the comfort of your home.

There are so many health benefits of cardiovascular exercise, some of which include a stronger heart and lungs, increased bone density, reduced stress, increased confidence, and better sleep.

I enjoy doing low intensity, aerobic exercise (jogging or cycling) in the morning on an empty stomach, as it allows my body to go into a "fat burning zone". I usually do this anywhere from 20-45 minutes, while making sure I spend at least 5 minutes warming up and cooling down.

I sometimes enjoy doing High Intensity Interval Training (HITT), but often only after having a meal in the morning as doing so on an empty stomach can risk the body burning muscle for fuel instead of fat.

There is nothing wrong with wanting a perfect beach body, but the next time that your willpower is low, think about all of the amazing ways that exercise is supporting your physical, mental, and emotional health.

Practice Deep Breathing

Our worlds have become so busy that we forget to engage in some of the simplest and most important things that support our health, like breathing.

The moment that you wake up in the morning, take a few long, deep breaths. This is a great way to relax the body, calm the mind, and ease your way into the day. Sounds simple, right?

Breathing is something that we do without thinking, unfortunately, many of us don't know how to do it correctly. Did you know that every process in your body depends on oxygen? When you engage in shallow breathing, this can cause a ton of stress on your organs.

Bad breathing habits, like shallow breathing, can give rise to a multitude of health problems, which is why it's so important to practice conscious breathing. The majority of your breathing should be done using your diaphragm.

From a physical perspective, it only takes three conscious diaphragmatic breaths to (a) reduce our blood pressure, pulse rate, and respiration rate, (b) cleanse the blood of lactate, and (c) generate alpha brain waves, which put us in "the zone."

Calm your mind by harnessing the power of your breath. Doing so will allow you to better manage any stress that you face throughout the day.

In the words of Eckhart Tolle, *"One conscious breath, in and out, is a meditation."*

A great book to read for mastering breathing is Just Breathe: Mastering Breathwork by Dan Brule.

Use PEMF Therapy

In today's world, sleep deprivation has become a universal phenomena, with modern technology being one of the primary culprits.

The blue light emitted by screens on cell phones, computers, tablets, and televisions restrain the production of melatonin, the hormone that controls your sleep/wake cycle or circadian rhythm. The result is undue stress on the cells of our body.

In order to master your day, it is imperative that you get a good night's sleep. This is where PEMF (Pulsed Electro-Magnetic Frequency) therapy mat can be very effective by laying on a PEMF mat daily.

Energy is everything. A PEMF mat is a portable mat that produces pulsed electromagnetic fields around an individual's body. This field then delivers healing energy to the body by producing negative ions and infrared waves. In terms of health benefits, the PEMF mat helps with the following:

- Decreases pain
- Improves post-surgery healing
- Improves sleep
- Regenerates nerves
- Enables relaxation and reduce stress
- Eliminates bodily toxins
- Reduces stress and fatigue

The PEMF mat brands and technology on the market that I like are:

The Bemer Group: http://projectlifemastery.com/bemer
Swiss Bionics Solutions:
http://projectlifemastery.com/swissbionics
EarthPulse: http://projectlifemastery.com/earthpulse

There is no easier way to improve your health at a cellular level. Give your cells the energy that they need in the morning so that you can function at an optimum level.

Do A Salt Water Flush

If you are someone that struggles with infrequent elimination, a salt water flush is the answer to your prayers. The purpose of a salt water flush is to help you cleanse your colon and digestive system. The result is a happy colon.

You may be wondering, "Why salt?" Salt is needed for many biochemical processes, including adrenal gland/thyroid gland function, cell wall stability, muscle contractions, nutrient absorption, nerve stimulation, pH, and water balance regulation.

Salt gives your digestive system the push that it needs in order to release the waste and toxins that are stored inside the body.

This colon cleansing process is one that has been practiced for years and is claimed to be a safe and effective way to cleanse your colon. Ditch the diuretics and pick up some salt.

When you give your colon the love that it needs, you can move throughout your day more freely!

Brush Teeth & Floss

Of all the things that are considered essential to health and wellbeing, one of the most underestimated is that of brushing your teeth and flossing. Your smile is your logo, so you want it to look good.

Brushing isn't enough, as this only removes the plaque on the surface of your teeth. Flossing is what helps remove plaque that is stuck between your teeth.

Because the mouth is an entry point for harmful bacteria to enter, research shows that having a healthy mouth reduces your risk for things like heart disease, diabetes, kidney problems, stroke, and even cancer.

It's recommend to brush at least twice a day with a natural toothpaste for at least two minutes, especially first thing in the morning and before bedtime. I always like to avoid ingesting chemicals whenever possible, hence using natural toothpaste.

Brushing and flossing every day not only gives you a beautiful smile, but it could also save your life!

Use A Neti Pot

The term nets pot originates from an ancient yogic technique of sinus rinsing, called Jala Neti.

We breathe in allergens and pollution every day, which can result in a buildup of mucus and toxins in our nose. This simple and inexpensive morning ritual is a great way to relieve yourself of the irritation that comes from colds, allergies, and sinus infections.

Two simple ingredients - purified water and salt travel - through the nasal membrane and work their magic. This is an allergy and sinus sufferer's dream. The health benefits of a *neti pot* include:

- Help to stop snoring
- Relief from sinus infections and cold symptoms, clear congested sinuses
- Enables deeper breathing
- Helps get rid of allergy symptoms

A study found that 87 percent of family doctors recommended saline nasal irrigation to their patients suffering from upper respiratory conditions such as chronic rhinosinusitis, seasonal allergic rhinitis, and viral upper respiratory infections.

You can usually find a Neti Pot at your local health foods store or on Amazon inexpensively.

Clear your sinuses so that you can start your day with a clear head!

Take A Cold Shower

It may feel energizing to start your day with a warm shower, but it actually has an opposite effect. Research shows that emerging from a hot shower into cooler air brings a sudden decrease in body temperature, leading to a tranquil state of mind. This is where the power of an icy cold shower comes into play.

It isn't easy jumping into what feels like pure ice, first thing in the morning, but that's why you should do it. What's great about hard things is that they make you stronger and more resilient.

If practiced on a daily basis, research shows that a cold shower can help with improved immunity and circulation, stress relief, better mood, fat loss, and relief of muscle soreness.

If you are ready to start your day with more energy and alertness, a cold shower is the way to go!

Take Supplements

Feeling at your best not only means eating right but also giving your body the nutrition that it needs for optimal wellbeing. If you want to get the maximum health benefits from supplements, it's important to understand what supplements you should take in the morning.

Taking a multivitamin in the morning, on a full stomach, is a great way to get the essential vitamins, minerals and antioxidants that you can't always get from food.

If you tend to feel sluggish in the mid-morning, ditch the coffee and try a B12 supplement, which will help with your energy levels and overall mood.

I always recommend for people to get a micronutrient test done to measure specific vitamins, minerals, antioxidants, amino/fatty acids and metabolites in your blood. This way you're not guessing and can ensure you're getting the nutrients you need through supplementation (ideally within your diet first, but supplements can make things easier).

Some of the supplements I take on a daily basis are:

- Multivitamins
- Minerals
- Vitamin C
- Vitamin D
- Vitamin B12
- Magnesium
- Digestive Enzymes
- Probiotics

I usually take more than this, based on if I'm doing a detox, recovering from a workout, or want to optimize my performance for the day. For example, sometimes I use nootropics like Alpha Brain by ONNIT to increase my focus or memory: http://projectlifemastery.com/alphabrain

It's always important to invest in quality supplements and brands - as most you find on the shelves are using poor quality ingredients and lack bioavailability for your body to fully absorb.

For example, for digestive enzyme and probiotics, I like a company called Bioptimizers: http://projectlifemastery.com/bioptimizers

Everyone will have different needs and goals. It's best to identify what you're deficient in and make sure you're covering all your bases, then try other supplements to further optimize your body and mental performance.

Taking supplements like these in the morning gives you the best chance that they will be absorbed into your system with the food that you eat throughout the day.

Your health is your wealth. If you take care of your body, it will take care of you.

Enjoy Red Light Therapy

Red light therapy has become the newest trend to hit the health and wellness world.
Red light therapy involves emitting red, low-light wavelengths through the skin to stimulate cellular

rejuvenation, increase blood flow, stimulate collagen and much more.

This form of therapy has been studied for decades now. It was first used by astronauts who were looking for effective ways to use light in order to grow plants in space.

A 2012 report published in Annals in Biomedical Engineering stated that red light is used in three primary ways:

- To reduce inflammation, edema, and chronic joint disorders
- To promote healing of wounds, deeper tissues, and nerves
- To treat neurological disorders and pain

However, the physical benefits of this therapy extend far beyond this. If you are ready to treat your skin, promote hair growth, or repair an injury, this is a safe and effective way to jumpstart your healing process!

I use the JOOVV red light therapy device, which you can learn more about at: http://projectlifemastery.com/joovv

Scrape Your Tongue

Tongue scraping is a an Ayurvedic self-care practice that has been around for years. It involves removing bacteria, food, fungi, toxins, and dead cells from the surface of the tongue.

Even though you may brush and floss your teeth in the morning, people forget about all the bacteria that lies on their tongues. Dental research has concluded that a tongue scraper is more effective at removing toxins and bacteria from the tongue than a toothbrush.

Scraping the best defense against bad breath, promotes good oral and digestive health, improves ability to taste, stimulates the internal organs, and helps to clear toxins and bacteria that live on the tongue.

It will surprise you how much stuff comes off of your tongue in the morning. Nobody likes morning breath. Start scraping!

Practice Oil Pulling

Oil pulling is an oral detoxification process that has been around for centuries, but it has started to gain a lot of popularity in the Western world. It is best done in the morning, on an empty stomach.

Simply take a tablespoon of oil (coconut or sesame), swish it around your mouth for at least 5 minutes, and spit it out. For those of you who have the time, 20 minutes is ideal. Timing is very important, as this is how long takes for the oil to break through plaque and bacteria.

Did you know that oil pulling is more effective than flossing your teeth?

Research shows that oil pulling is one of the most effective natural health solutions for preventing tooth decay and loss, reducing inflammation, boosting the immune system, preventing heart disease, improving skin conditions, whitening teeth, and healing bleeding gums.

Due to it's antibacterial and antiviral properties, oil pulling has the potential to heal almost anything on or in the body. Ditch the mouthwash and reach for some oil instead. Your health will thank you for it.

Juicing

If you find yourself feeling lethargic throughout the day or have the desire to cleanse your body of toxins, juicing is a great way to give your body the vitamins and minerals that it needs for the whole day.

Ninety-five percent of the vitamins that our bodies need are found in the juice of raw fruits and vegetables.

Juicing has a range of health benefits, some of which include:

- Helping with digestion
- Detoxifying the body
- Providing more energy

- Providing brain power
- Acting as a natural stress reliever

It's important to keep in mind that you should avoid buying bottled juices from the store as oftentimes they are filled with sugar and have been pasteurized in order to ensure that they last longer.

Juices should always be fresh, raw, organic and ideally cold-pressed.

Avoid juicing fruit if possible, due to the high concentrated sugar content. I like to keep my juices as mostly green vegetables, then add in beets, carrots, ginger and lemon to improve the taste. Sometimes I'll add in some fruit, such as apple or pineapple, but only in small amounts.

Cold-pressed, masticating juicers are typically better than juice extractors, as they help preserve the nutrients and you typically get more juice out of the vegetables.

Make juicing a part of your daily life. I remember my mentor Jim Rohn once said: *"If you can't afford a juicer, then sell your car. A juicer will get you further in life!"*

There is no better way to improve your overall health and energy levels.

Practice Rebounding

Rebounding on a mini-trampoline is a fun way to start your day. A rebounder applies weight and movement to every cell, causing the entire body to be strong, more flexible, and healthier.

Research by NASA hows that rebounding can be more than twice as effective as treadmill running.

Rebounding has unique benefits compared to other forms of exercise because it involves increasing our G-force.

G-force refers to the force created on the body as a result of acceleration or gravity. When you jump on a rebounder, you initially bounce upward, pause for less than a second at a point where you are weightless, then the G-force (the force that causes you to come back down to the surface of the trampoline) increases during the downward motion.

The health benefits of rebounding include:

- Increased energy and endurance
- Increased strength and muscle tone
- Improved flexibility
- Improved digestion and elimination
- Improved circulation and toxin elimination
- Stimulates your lymphatic system
- Increases white blood cells by up to 3 times

- Aids in weight loss
- Heart health
- Reduced back pain
- Stress management
- Balance and agility

I personally like to bounce on a rebounder in the morning while I'm doing some of the rituals for my Mind, mentioned later in this book. The biggest benefit I get is a huge energy boost, which allows me to kickstart the day.

Just like with anything, it's important to invest in a quality rebounder. Buying a a cheap rebounder can actually have negative affects on your spinal cord, can easily break or cause injury.

I personally like and use the Cellerciser by David Hall, which folds up for traveling:
https://projectlifemastery.com/rebounder

Integrating this activity into your morning ritual will transform your overall health and wellbeing.

What are you waiting for? Start bouncing!

Dry Brush Your Skin

We all brush our teeth and hair, but how often do you brush your skin? Dry brushing is a quick and easy wellness practice that costs nothing and helps cleanse your body from the inside out. According to naturopath, Dr. Denice Moffat, *"The skin is also known as the third kidney."*

Dry brushing offers multiple benefits, some of which include: stimulating your lymphatic system, exfoliation, increasing circulation, reducing cellulite, stimulating the sweat glands, and improving digestion and kidney function.

The best time to brush is before your morning shower, which is a great way to energize your body before your day begins. Start at your feet and work your way up the body, brushing in circular motions towards your heart.

Don't make this a daily routine because it can be hard on the skin. Rather, focus on brushing 2-3 times/week. There is no better way to get soft and glowing skin. Start brushing!

Drink A Smoothie

While juicing is a great way to absorb a lot of vitamins and minerals in your bloodstream, the downside is that you're missing out on the fibre which is important for digestion. That's why drinking a smoothie that contains fruits, vegetables, good fats and protein is a great way to get the boost that you need to have a full-power morning.

The health benefits of drinking smoothies made with fruits and vegetables that are rich in vitamins and minerals include:

- Reduces cravings
- Improves digestion
- Boosts your immunity
- Supports weight loss
- Improves hydration
- Gives your skin a healthy glow

For example, a smoothie with kale in it is a great way to cleanse your liver and strengthen your blood. Plus, it will keep you feeling energized all day.

Plus, combining super nutritious ingredients, like cucumber or spinach, with tasty flavors, like mango or cacao, is a beautifully colorful way to enjoy your breakfast.

You can be creative and add superfoods, along with other nutritious ingredients, which will help support your body for the day.

I personally love using the Vitamix blender for making smoothies: http://projectlifemastery.com/vitamix

Dancing

There is no better way to start your day than moving your body to your favorite song. Dancing is healing in motion. It is using our bodies as medicine, allowing for the movement of stuck energy.

Research shows that dancing may help the healing process as a person gains a sense of control through mastery of movement, and works as an escape from stress and pain through a change in emotion and/or physical capability.

Dancing means letting go and allowing oneself to unapologetically and freely express yourself without reservations. It's about letting the rhythm take over us, bringing out our youthful, playful side.

Spend the morning connecting to your intuitive self and have fun in the process. No matter what is going on inside or around you, dancing allows you forget about the world; it puts you in the present moment, which is where the purest form of joy resides.

In the words of Jacques d'Amboise, *"Dance is your pulse, your heartbeat, your breathing. It's the rhythm of your life."*

Coffee Enemas

If you are looking for a way to cleanse your colon and give your liver the detox that it deserves, a coffee enema is the way to go. During the process, a mixture of brewed, caffeinated coffee and warm water is inserted into the colon through the rectum.

Coffee enemas stimulate bile flow and the production of glutathione by up to 700%. Glutathione is one of the body's master antioxidants that is involved in different phases of detoxification.

If you can hold a coffee enema for 15 minutes, you will achieve the full benefits that come with it, some of which include removal of intestinal parasites, yeast overgrowth, and heavy metals from the body.

It may sound crazy and some may be slightly skeptical, but enemas have been a common detox process that has been around for thousands of years and were even written about in the Dead Sea Scrolls.

I've personally have benefited from doing coffee enemas a few times per week and have noticed incredible results.

You can even try wheatgrass enemas and other types, which also have great health benefits.

You can find Enema Kits at a local health food store or on Amazon.

By cleansing your body of toxins in your colon, you will feel a greater sense of mental clarity, better sleeps, and increased energy levels.

Laughing

An easy way to live a happier and healthier life is to laugh more. Many of us take life too seriously and forget to enjoy the simple pleasures in life.

What do you think would happen if we took a different approach to challenges in our lives and actually laughed our way through them, instead of getting stressed and overwhelmed?

Well, science is proving that laughter actually is the best medicine and a great coping mechanism against negative emotions. Research shows that laughter strengthens your immune system, boosts mood, diminishes pain, and protects you from the damaging effects of stress.

Sometimes in the morning, I force myself to smile and laugh out loud. In the beginning it seems a bit forced, but then once you start laughing you soon get momentum and it starts to feel good.

To make things easier, think of a funny moment that made you laugh in your life, or turn on a funny video.

Never underestimate the power of a good laugh. Integrate it into your morning routine and watch how it has the ability to transform your entire day, and your life.

In the words of Charlie Chaplin, *"A day without laughter is a day wasted."*

Take A Wheatgrass Shot

Many people swear by taking a shot of wheatgrass every morning.

Wheatgrass is rich in the following nutrients - chlorophyll, iron, vitamin C, A, E, antioxidants, selenium, and electrolytes, including magnesium and calcium.

Referred to as "liquid sunshine" because of its high chlorophyll content, the health benefits of wheatgrass are abundant, some of which include the following:

- Stimulates circulation
- Improves immunity
- Reduces fatigue
- Eliminates body odor
- Cleanses the liver
- Prevents cancer

Wheatgrass is a powerful detoxifier, so it is important that you ease into it by taking one ounce, and gradually upping it to two ounces per day.

This is enough to provide you with all of the energy that you will need for the entire day.

Wheatgrass is one of the best superfoods. Be kind to your body and give it the fuel that it needs in order to crush your day!

Practice Wim Hof's Breathing Technique

The Wim Hof method is a powerful deep breathing meditation that was developed by a Dutch man named Wim Of, otherwise referred to others as, "the iceman."

He is best known for running shirtless above the Arctic Circle and diving under the ice at the North Pole. By exposing himself to the harsh conditions of nature, he learned to tolerate the intense forces of cold and heat, mastering his mindset in the process.

His breathing technique involves 30 deep, rhythmic inhales through your nose and exhales through your mouth, followed by holding your breath.

In 2014, a study in the Proceedings of the National Academy of Sciences found that people could learn to control their immune responses and autonomous nervous system after just ten days of Hof's breathing exercises and meditation.

Wake up every day and practice Hof's breathing technique, and over time watch your life change for the better. This is an easy and effective way to master your mind, body, and soul.

To learn more about Wim Hof's techniques, check out his book The Way Of The Iceman: How The Wim Hof Method Creates Radiant, Longterm Health.

Drink Something Green

Before you eat anything in the morning, I encourage you to drink something green.

As I've already mentions, wheatgrass, green juices and smoothies are the best ways to enjoy some of the benefits of greens.

However, if you can't accomplish any of these, I like to supplement with greens in powder form, which I can easily mix with water.

This is a great way to fill your body with an abundance of vitamins and minerals. Trust me when I say that this will give you a great energy boost to jumpstart your day.

Some of the health benefits of having a daily green drink include improvement of gut health, immune system support, weight loss, improved energy, and glowing skin.

One of my favorite brands is called Athletic Greens, which you can learn more about here: http://projectlifemastery.com/athleticgreens

Weigh Yourself

Taking charge of your health and well-being is important to living a happy and well-balanced life. The best way to do this is through regular exercise and lift weighting, as well as regularly checking your body weight.

For example, if one of your goals is to lose five pounds of body fat, the act of weighing yourself is an important and useful measure of your progress. A number of studies and review articles have demonstrated that daily self-weighing is associated with better long-term management of weight.

Weighing yourself every morning provides instant feedback regarding how your current behavior is impacting your weight. This is a great way to make sure that you are on track with your goals, so that you can adjust your workout or diet, if you aren't moving in the right direction.

As long as you view the number that you see on the scale as a motivator, rather than a measure of your worth, weighing yourself every day can be beneficial.

As Steve Maraboli said, "The scale can ONLY tell you what you weigh; not who you are."

Use A Sun Light Therapy Light

If you don't live in a sunny climate all year round, naturally your body won't get as much natural light. On top of that, a lot of people spend their days exposed to artificial light, whether that's looking at their computer screens or being indoors.

Not getting enough natural light can affect your sleep, mood and overall cognitive functioning. The good news is that it is possible to feel energized, no matter what the sky looks like. This is where a sun light therapy light can come in handy.

These special lights are designed to mimic outdoor light, helping to improve your mood and ease other symptoms of the "winter blues."

It can also help relieve circadian sleep disorders, shift work adjustment, jet lag and low energy. It is safe, natural and effective.

You have the power to restore your body's natural circadian rhythm and bring more light into your life.

Keep in mind that, if you have skin or eye sensitivities, I encourage you to check with your doctor before using a sun light therapy device.

Note: It's most ideal to go outside and go outside immediately upon waking in the morning, but if that's not an option, this is a great solution for you. There's some great ones available on Amazon.

MIND

In order to get the most out of your day and life, you must stimulate and expand your mind.

Your thoughts, feelings and beliefs will determine the actions and behaviors you take in your life. Your mind is like a muscle, you can train and condition it to help support the life you want.

That's why it's important to include some of these habits in your morning first, first thing upon waking. By turning on your mind, it'll allow you to tap more into your potential for the day.

Below are some of my favorite rituals for your mind.

Recite Affirmations

Self-affirmations are a powerful tool for personal growth and development. Reciting empowering and uplifting affirmations that remind you of your unlimited potential is a great way to start your day.

Not only that, but the act of saying them out loud energizes you to take massive action towards achieving your goals so that you can be one step closer to living the life you have always dreamed of.

A study published in the Journal of Personality and Social Psychology found that self-affirmations can improve willpower and self-control by providing individuals with an extra boost in motivation. Your identity is the sum of your beliefs about who you are.

Phrases like, *"I am capable of doing and being anything"* condition your mind to focus on positive and uplifting thoughts about yourself and your abilities.

The result? Your internal motivation and confidence skyrockets.

When you shift your mindset, your whole life changes. Quiet your mind by integrating affirmations into your daily ritual.

Every thought and every word you say creates your life experiences.

Choose wisely.

In the words of Buddha, *"What you think, you become."*

A great book to learn more about the power of affirmations is What You Say When You Talk To Yourself by Shad Helmstetter.

Meditation

If you want to be productive, you need to start off the day with a calm, clear head.

In today's turbocharged world, where your attention is pulled in multiple different directions at once, it is more important than ever to train your mind to focus and relax.

The best way to do that is by taking some time every morning to honor yourself by going inward and enjoying some stillness. Studies have shown that meditating, just ten minutes a day, reduces stress, lowers cortisol levels, and improves your outlook on life.

Most people make the mistake of thinking that they have to meditate for hours in lotus position in order to achieve any results, but this is far from true.

Develop your own personal style. Sit in a position that you are comfortable with, and listen to music if that helps to calm your mind.

Here are a few examples of how meditation can improve your life:

- Reduces stress
- Improves concentration
- Increases self-awareness
- Increases happiness
- Benefits cardiovascular and immune health
- Lessens anxiety

Take a few minutes every day to breathe, be still, and go inward.

Kris Carr said it best, *"Your mind is your sovereign space and you are the leader of that kingdom."*

Today, there's some incredible apps and devices that can help us optimize our meditation experience and make it more enjoyable.

My favorite is using the Muse, which helps to track your brainwaves while meditating and helps you get into a calm state: http://projectlifemastery.com/muse

Reading

Stimulating your mind with positive and empowering ideas is a great way to wake up your brain in the morning. When we read a good book, it allows our minds to wander into different worlds and inspires us to question how and why things are the way they are.

Reading is also a meditative practice which allows you to calm your mind and focus your energies on the pages in front of you.

The most successful people in the world commit to personal growth and development. They have a passionate curiosity for learning.

Warren Buffett was once asked about the secret to his success in finance. He replied, *"Read 500 pages like this every day. That's how knowledge works. It builds up, like compound interest."*

Even if it's only 10 pages, spend some time every morning filling your mind with positive words that uplift you.

If you read 10 pages a day, that'd be 300 pages per month, which is roughly one book per month.

Here are 25 books that changed my life:
https://projectlifemastery.com/25-books-that-changed-my-life/

Recite Your Mission Statement

Do you have a personal mission statement that reflects your deepest desires for your future self?

If not, it's time to write one.

Writing and reciting your mission statement out loud every morning is a call to action; it's a powerful reminder of what your core values are and what your purpose in life is.

There are three main steps to building your personal mission statement: *define, disseminate and demonstrate.* This is a way of getting in touch with yourself and discovering what it is that's most important to you.

First, start by asking yourself what your core values are, then share your mission statement with others, and lastly, demonstrate it in action.

If you are not living in alignment with your mission, this activity will inspire you to get back on track.

Who are you and what do you want to contribute to the world?

As motivational speaker Zig Ziglar once said, *"Outstanding people have one thing in common: An absolute sense of mission."*

Practice Gratitude

Gratitude is the key to living a life of happiness, and one of the most important rituals that you can practice every day.

It has been scientifically proven that expressing gratitude may be one of the simplest ways to feel better, and it also helps in improving physical and psychological health.

Start your day by being thankful for what you have, instead of dwelling on what is missing. When you focus on the good, more good things come to you.

In his book, "Thanks! How Practicing Gratitude Can Make You Happier", UC Davis researcher, Dr. Robert Emmons says that being thankful actually amplifies the good.

Write down 3 things that you are grateful for every morning. When you do so, it helps you focus on the positive in your life.

Expressing words of gratitude on paper is a great way to reprogram your brain because it teaches you that positive behavior matters.

In the words of Marcus Aurelius, "*When you arise in the morning, think of what a precious privilege it is to be alive – to breathe, to think, to enjoy, to love.*"

Ask Yourself Empowering Questions

The whole purpose of having a morning ritual is to empower you to take responsibility for your life.

Do you want to know the secret for getting what you want in life?

If you want to create a real shift in your life, ask empowering questions.

In his book, "Awaken The Giant Within", Tony Robbins expressed that by consistently asking yourself these types of questions, you will be able to access your most empowering emotional states on a regular basis, like joy, gratitude, and love.

Empowering questions have the power to direct your mindset and your focus to what you want most in life. They invite you to look inside yourself and reflect on what is important.

Here's some empowering questions you can ask yourself every morning:

- What am I grateful for in my life right now?
- What am I happy about in my life right now?
- What am I excited about in my life right now?
- What am I proud of in my life right now?
- What am I passionate about in my life right now?
- What am I committed to in my life right now?
- Who do I love and who loves me?

If you have difficulties thinking of answers to these, try asking instead: *"What COULD I feel grateful for in my life right now?"*

Remember to really focus on the feelings and amplifying it. One way you can do this is by asking the follow-up question, *"How does this make me feel?"*

Keep in mind that the way you frame your questions determines the process by which you search for the answers.

Dr. Wayne Dyer suggests that, rather than asking, "Why me?" which is a disempowering question, ask yourself, "What can I learn from this experience and what steps can I take in order to make this work for me?"

In essence, the quality of our questions determine the quality of our lives.

In the words of Warren Berger, *"A beautiful question shifts the way we think about something and often sets in motion a process than can result in change."*

Are you ready to ask your way to a better life?

Listen To An Audiobook Or Podcast

With the rise of mobile devices and tablets becoming commonplace in today's digital world, audiobooks and podcasts are fast becoming the new trend.

While reading a physical book requires a deeper level of concentration, audiobooks and podcasts allow for multitasking; they are something that you can listen to while you are driving or exercising at the gym.

Not only that, audiobooks and podcasts can help you get through content faster, and depending on the nature of the material, can be soothing.

New research shows that audiobooks have a powerful impact on literacy development as well. Listening to an audiobook or podcast is an easy and effective way to accelerate your learning and expand your mind, on your terms.

Put in some headphones, read through your ears, and listen to something every morning that inspires you to live your best life.

Check out my Project Life Mastery podcast to consume my inspirational audio contentt:
http://projectlifemastery.com/podcast

Watch An Inspiring Video

There is no better way to motivate and energize yourself and to stay committed to your path, than by watching an inspiring video in the morning.

Inspiring videos remind us of the importance of living in accordance with our highest selves.

On days when you feel like giving up, they can remind you of your 'why', offering words that ease your mind and propel you towards taking massive action.

Sometimes, listening to someone else's words can be all that you need in order to boost your confidence and shift your mindset from one that is disempowering to one that is empowering.

In one study, Penn State researchers found that those who watched inspiring videos felt more elevation, and therefore felt a greater connection to humanity overall, across different races and ethnicities.

No matter where you are on your journey to success, if you want to master your psychology and improve your life, start your day watching an inspiring video.

When you expand your mind, you unlock the unlimited potential that resides within you. One video could change your life.

In the words of Zig Ziglar, *"You never know when a moment and a few sincere words could have an impact on your life forever."*

Check out my Project Life Mastery YouTube channel to consume my inspirational video content:
http://projectlifemastery.com/youtube

Listen to Binaural Beats

In our 24/7 world, finding ways to relax and calm our busy minds is more important than ever before. Coined a *digital drug*, binaural beats are a brainwave entrainment technology designed to put your brain into the same activity state as when you are meditating.

Ancient cultures have been using the power of consistent, rhythmic sounds for thousands of years, although they didn't call it binaural beats.

Binaural beats were first brought into modern day awareness by a biophysicist named Dr. Gerald Oster, who concluded that, *"It is possible that hormonally induced physiological behavior changes may be made apparent by measuring the binaural-beat spectrum."*

For those of you who struggle with meditation, this is great alternative. One study found that using these technologies, including binaural beats, was beneficial for the following:

- Anger
- Anxiety
- Memory
- Sleep
- Depression

All you need to do is put on a pair of headphones in the morning and let your brain waves synchronize with the relaxing sounds. It's that easy!

Write and Read Out Goals

When was the last time that you sat down and actually wrote down what it is that you want to achieve in life?

The simple act of writing down your goals gives you clarity and reminds you of the specific actions that you need to take in order to get to where you want to be.

According to a study done by Gail Matthews at Dominican University, those who write down their goals accomplish significantly more than those who do not.

Not only do you need to write your goals down, but in order to manifest them, you need to read them out loud.

The power of intention cannot be understated. When it comes to achieving your goals, you need to harness the power of your unconscious mind and feed it with inspiring information.

The combination of saying your goals out loud with emotion, and repeating those messages on a consistent basis is the key to getting maximum results from your subconscious mind.

In the words of Bryant McGill, *"A goal that is not written is not a goal. It only becomes real when you write it down...let your list of goals become a mantra and a meditation."*

One of my favorite goal setting programs is The 100 Day Challenge by Gary Ryan Blair:
http://projectlifemastery.com/100daychallenge

Create A Vision Board

A vision board is a powerful visualization tool for manifesting your goals and dreams. What does your ideal life look like?

Scientists have found that thinking about a goal is just as important as doing an action toward a goal.

Keep in mind that your vision board should reflect how you want to *feel* as much as what you want.

The Law of Attraction states that what we focus on, expands. When you are engaging in the process of visualization, you are sending a message to the Universe that says, "This is what I want", and in turn the Universe listens.

Successful people have been using vision boards for years.

Jack Canfield, the New York Times Bestselling Author of the "Chicken Soup For The Soul" book series, says,

"Creating a vision board is probably one of the most valuable visualization tools available to you."

Find positive images that inspire and motivate you to wake up every day and take the steps towards living the life that you desire.

A great book on the law of attraction is The Secret by Rhonda Byrne.

Find An Accountability Buddy

How many goals have you set for yourself that you failed to achieve for seemingly no reason? Staying committed to your goals can be challenging at times, which is why it's helpful to have an accountability buddy.

It's a lot more difficult to back out of doing something that you promised to do when backing out will undoubtedly disappoint that someone.

The American Society of Training and Development (ASTD) did a study on accountability and found the following statistics:

The probability of completing a goal if:

- You *have* an idea or a goal: 10%
- You *consciously decide* you will do it: 25%
- You decide *when* you will do it: 40%

- You *plan how* you will do it: 50%
- You *commit to someone* you will do it: 65%
- You have a *specific accountability appointment* with a person you've committed to: **95%**

The numbers speak for themselves. We all need an empowering ecosystem, a group of positive, successful people that take massive action.

By hopping on a 10-minute call in the morning with an accountability buddy, you can share with them what you're committed to achieving for that day and keep each other accountable to following through.

Find an accountability buddy with whom you can celebrate your accomplishments with, express your challenges, and receive critical feedback and support in all areas of your life. When you do so, it will ensure that you begin your day with a calm, proactive, and focused mindset.

Sometimes it only takes one person who can change your life.

In the words of the late Steven Covey, *"Accountability breeds response-ability."*

Who are you accountable to?

Never forget that there is strength in numbers. If you don't have an accountability buddy yet, it's time to find one.

Visualization

The power of visualization cannot be ignored. It is what turns dreams into reality. It all starts with your mind.

Imagine that you could go from living in the energetic space that you currently reside in, and shift to a happier, more fulfilled, and successful life?

You can.

The trick is to start imagining that it is already your reality.

Research has found that daily mental practices can enhance motivation, increase confidence and self-efficacy, prime your brain for success, and increase states of flow – all of which support you in the achievement of your best life.

When you wake up every morning BELIEVE that at the core of your being, all that which you are trying to achieve.

In your mind's eye, see yourself actually moving throughout your day, doing what you love to do. What would it look like?

When you do so, you will be begin to experience the emotions associated with that event and begin to feel what it would feel like if that event were to actually transpire.

You have the power to do and be anything.

Don't wait for success to come to you. Simply close your eyes and visualize it happening.

If you do this every day, eventually you will open your eyes and see that you are actually living your dream.

In the words of Richard Brach, *"To bring anything into your life, imagine that it is already there."*

To learn more about the power of visualization, check out the book Psycho-Cybernetics by Maxwell Maltz.

Plan Out Your Day

If you want to have a highly productive day and crush your goals, you need to know what such a day would look like and then plan to make that day a reality.

Planning requires self-discipline and commitment. There are a limited number of hours in the day and if you lead a busy life, your success in accomplishing your goals will be determined by your ability to effectively prioritize.

Think of a plan as if it were a prioritization tool. In doing so, you will be able to know which things need to be completed, versus those things that can wait.

My favorite daily planning tool is called the EVO Planner, which is custom-tailored to the individual based on your brain type to help you get into a flow state.

I've used many daily planning methods in the past, but found that there's no one-size-fits-all solution that works for everyone. We all have different brain-types and ways for us to get into flow and experience peak productivity.

There's a free brain-assessment you can take through EVO, which you can learn more about here:
https://projectlifemastery.com/evoassessment

To check out the EVO Planner, go here:
http://projectlifemastery.com/evo

Otherwise, ANY planning and scheduling is better than nothing - even if you use a "to do list". Even though "to do lists" are fairly old-school and not the most effective approach, you're at least being proactive each day!

If you haven't been able to make progress or achieve your goals, it's time to start planning. Remember to focus on the highest leverage tasks first and not get caught up in the menial tasks that don't result in much progress in your life.

In the words of Stephen Keague, *"Proper planning and preparation prevents poor performance."*

Make Your Bed

This may seem like a simple task, but making your bed actually sets the tone for how the rest of your day will unfold.

Why?

Because it reinforces the fact that the small things in life are what create the biggest results in the long-run.

William McRaven, a four-star commander and author of the best-selling book, "Make Your Bed: Little Things That Can Change Your Life... And Maybe the World", believes that making your bed might be tedious and repetitive to some people, but it can provide a boost for your day.

I believe that our future successes are determined by our daily choices.

Making your bed is a choice; it represents an act of discipline.

At the end of a busy day, it's a reminder that you had done something well. Not only that, but it's nice to come home to a clean room and bed, especially if you've had a bad day.

Tim Ferriss best describes the value of making your bed every morning - *"In my life... there's a lot of uncertainty,"* Ferriss explains, but *"no matter how shitty your day is, no matter how catastrophic it might become, you can make your bed, and that gives me the feeling even in a disastrous day that I've held on by a fingernail."*

Focus On Your Highest Leverage Activity

Starting your day with your highest leverage activity that utilizes your strengths is the best way to guarantee that you will achieve the greatest results.

A high leverage activity, as defined by Gary Keller, is *"The one thing that you can do, such that by doing it, everything else will be easier or unnecessary."*

It doesn't matter how productive you are, if you aren't focusing on the right things, you won't accomplish anything.

The best way to wrap your head around the concept of leverage is to look at the 80/20 Pareto Principle which states that 80% of our results come from 20% of our efforts. Your efforts represent your highest leverage activities.

Stop spending time on tasks that are of low value and that somebody else could do.

In the words of Gay Hendricks, "*Your zone of genius is usually where your highest leverage activities tend to lie. These tend to be the things that nobody could do but you.*"

Reading Quotes

Reading inspiring quotes is a great way to lift yourself out of bed every morning and prime your mind for greatness.

Why?

Because positive words lead to positive thinking.

Research shows that positive emotions broaden your sense of possibilities and open your mind, which in turn allows you to build new skills that can provide value in all areas of your life.

Uplifting words give us the space to dream big, spark change, and inspire us to keep moving forward and take action towards the achievement of our goals.

Scott Sobel, the Founder of Media & Communications Strategies, Inc. argues that the interest in reading inspirational quotes may be rooted in biology, saying that, *"Humans are aspirational. We want to look up to role models and leaders, and follow what they ask... leaders and their inspirational quotes affect us on a primal level."*

Quotes are great reminders of what is most important to us and they have the power to inspire how our day unfolds.

I personally like to write them out on flash cards and read a few of them out loud each day, similar to an affirmation.

Find words that move and resonate with you, and recite them out loud to yourself every day.

Listen to Uplifting Music

How does it make you feel when your favorite song comes on the radio?

For most of us, it stimulates our emotions and tunes us into a more positive outlook on life.

Music has been scientifically proven to uplift people's emotions. If you have difficulty meditating, listening to music is a great alternative.

Choose a song that brings out the emotions that you want to feel throughout the day, and listen to it repeatedly.

In her book, "On Repeat: How Music Plays the Mind", psychologist Elizabeth Hellmuth Margulis explains why listening to music on repeat improves focus. When you do so, you tend to *dissolve* into the song, which blocks out 'mind wandering.'

A study from the University of Missouri suggests that listening to music when you're angry or sad provides an instant boost to your mood.

In the words of Bob Marley, *"One good thing about music is that when it hits you, you feel no pain."*

Read Your Life Vision Out Loud

A vision is what helps you achieve your goals and dreams in life.

What would your best life look like?

Give yourself permission to dream big. When you know what you want your future to look like, it motivates you to take action.

Research has found that a person can experience leisure in anything. Your work can become your leisure. When you are passionate about something, it no longer feels like a job but instead, it feels like a hobby that excites and inspires you.

What is it that makes you want to get out of bed each and every morning?

Once you write your vision statement, you need to make it a reality. If you need some extra motivation, read your vision out loud to yourself.

This is a great opportunity to get out of your head and into your heart.

Write down a list of emotions that your vision incites in you when you say it out loud. This is a great way to inspire you to take action and stick with the plan that you set out for yourself.

In the words of Oprah Winfrey, *"Create the highest, grandest vision possible for your life because you become what you believe."*

Journaling

Have you ever found it hard to express how you feel?

Journaling is a great exercise to remove mental blocks and clarify your thoughts and feelings, especially first thing in the morning.

Research confirms that the brain, specifically the prefrontal cortex, is most active and readily creative immediately following sleep.

Journaling allows you to access your inner world and helps you get to know yourself better and what is most important to you.

There is increasing evidence to support the notion that journaling has a positive impact on physical well-being.

A number of studies have shown that writing about what you are grateful for in your journal, rather than focusing on frustrations, can improve your health, your sense of well-being, and boosts your immunity.

Pick up a pen and piece of paper and making journaling a regular morning habit. This is your time to get honest with yourself and freely express how you feel.

In the words of J.M. Barrie, *"The life of every man is a diary in which he means to write one story, and writes another; and his humblest hour is when he compares the volume as it is with what he vowed to make it."*

Emotional Flood

Gratitude is a powerful force that can transform every area of our lives.

Developed by Tony Robbins, the emotional flood exercise is an easy and effective way to experience an overwhelming amount of happiness, joy and gratitude, in just five minutes.

Research by renowned psychologists Robert Emmons and Michael McCullough found that people who consciously focus on gratitude experience and gain the following:

- Feel optimistic about the future

- Get sick less often

- Exercise more regularly

- Have more energy, enthusiasm, determination, and focus

- Make greater progress toward achieving important personal goals

- Sleep better and wake up feeling refreshed

When you start your day feeling grateful for your life, it overpowers any negative emotions that may pop into your head, filling your heart with joy and happiness.

The process is simple.

Put on some inspiring music, close your eyes, and ask yourself these questions:

- What is a moment from my life when I felt happiness and joy?

- What is a moment from my life of gratitude?

- What is a fun moment from my life?

- What is a playful moment from my life?

- What is a moment in my life where I felt proud of myself?

- What is a sexy or sensual moment from my life?

- What is a moment in my life where I felt guided?

- What is a moment with friends, family or loved ones?

The goal is to ask these questions a few times, stacking them over and over again, so that you're flooding yourself with all of these incredible memories from your life.

Once you've done that for a few minutes, you can then start to flood yourself with moments from the future that are yet to come. This allows you to tap into your imagination, as a preview of your life's coming attractions.

- What is a happy moment that is yet to come in my future?

- What is a moment in my future where I'll feel grateful?

- What is a moment in my future where I will feel proud?

- What is a moment in my future of fun and adventure?

- What is a sexy and sensual moment to come in my future?

- What is a moment in my future of success or accomplishment?

Really make sure you feel the emotions and take it all in. Use your mind to visualize and make it as real as possible.

By doing the emotional flood exercise each day, it will allow you to reprogram your brain to experience a flood of emotions of love, gratitude, and happiness.

Use NLP To Anchor Emotional States

Our emotional state has the power to impact our behavior. Emotions don't happen to us. Rather, we create them, based on our perceptions of the world.

Many people are victims to their emotions and believe that they don't have any control over how they feel. This is far from true. You are in charge of your mind and you can change the meaning that you ascribe to any event.

Our success in life is determined, in part, by our ability to master our emotions. A great approach for learning how to master your emotional state is neuro-euro-linguistic programming (NLP) which is an approach to communication and personal development that explores how we think and feel.

The NLP technique makes use of anchors for inducing positive emotional states in people, like happiness or relaxation. The idea behind using this technique is for an individual to build up a resource of positive emotional states that can be harnessed in any situation where they are needed.

Here's how it works:

You first want to put yourself in a resourceful state (happiness, confidence, gratitude, excitement, etc...), which is easy to do following some of the techniques mentioned earlier in this book (empowering questions, emotional flood, etc...).

When you're in that resourceful state, you want to do something unique with frequency to anchor that emotion to it.

For example, when you're feeling happy and excited, you could clench your right fist and say "Yes!" out loud.

If you do this enough times, the emotional state of happiness and excitement will become linked (or anchored) to the gesture of clenching your right fist and saying "Yes!"

This is useful, because you could use fire off this anchor anytime you want to - when you're feeling sad, depressed, unmotivated, or lazy. Just clench your right fist and say "Yes!" and you'll instantly start feeling happiness and excitement.

A successful anchor requires emotional intensity and frequency, as it's a new pattern that you're conditioning. But once set up properly, it's incredibly powerful.

Having the ability to anchor yourself and change your state of mind in the midst of life's challenges, has the power to transform your entire day.

To learn more about NLP, check out the work by co-founders Richard Bandler and John Grinder.

Reflect On Your Life Values And What's Most Important To You

The decisions that we make in life are reflective of our values.

Our values represent the core aspects that make up who we are.

What do you stand for?

What's most important to you in your life?

John C. Maxwell said it best: *"Your core values are the deeply held beliefs that authentically describe your soul."*

The process of identifying your life values involves a discovery of what you are passionate about, as well as what is important to you.

If you don't know what is important to you, how can you expect to have a meaningful and fulfilling life?

Living in your truth means that your actions and words are in alignment with your core life values.

Keep in mind that your values can shift over time. It is an ongoing process of discovery based upon the events that unfold in your life.

Nevertheless, making the commitment to wake up every day and live in alignment with your truth will ignite your passion and give you the utmost joy and fulfillment in life.

SPIRIT

While mastering our body and mind is extremely important, we can't neglect what is most important: our spirit.

We're all spiritual beings.

As Pierre Teihard de Chardin said: "We are not human beings have a spiritual experience, we are spiritual beings having a human experience."

By connecting with our spirit each day, we'll access more of who we truly are, which will lead to deeper fulfillment and meaning in our lives.

Below are some of my favorite rituals for your spirit.

Express Gratitude

Expressing gratitude is one of the most powerful communication tools.

Gratitude helps us connect to something larger than ourselves, whether that means to other people, nature, or a higher power.

Start your day by taking a moment and thinking about one person who has shaped and changed your life for the better.

Next, reach out to that person and express gratitude to them. Either call them on the phone, send them a text message, e-mail or better yet tell them in-person.

Nothing says, *"I appreciate you"* more than sending a message of gratitude to someone in your life that has brought you joy.

When someone feels heard, they in turn show gratitude back to you.

When you express gratitude, you automatically increase the power of your recognition.

In 2014, Mark Zuckerberg challenged himself to writing a thank-you note every day. If he has the time to do it, so do you.

In the words of Voltaire, *"Appreciation is a wonderful thing. It makes what is excellent in others belong to us as well."*

Practice Forgiveness

We all have built up resistance and resentment towards others.

We've had people lie to us, hurt us, or even abused us.

The pain and resentment we hold onto from these experiences can affect our ability to love others and be happy.

Holding onto resentment is a source of suffering for many. The only way to be free from this pain is to learn how to let it go by forgiving.

As Nelson Mandela said, "Resentment is like drinking poison and then hoping it will kill your enemies."

It's important to understand that no matter how justified your resentment may be, that it's causing suffering in your life, whether you're consciously aware of it or not.

Forgiveness is more for ourselves, than the other person.

It requires courage to raise your level of consciousness as a human being and decide to let go of the pain, resentment, and choose to forgive.

One of the best ways you can do this is to try to turn the negatives of your life into a positive.

If someone hurt you in the past, look at how this could be a gift in your life - perhaps it made you a more caring and sensitive person?

Maybe the hurt you experienced forced you to develop yourself as a human being and become more?

What good has resulted from this pain? If you look hard enough, you can find a positive aspect of it to appreciate.

It's about remembering that everything in your life happens for a reason and a purpose, and it serves you. It's up to you to find out what that meaning was and use it to your advantage.

I believe that life doesn't happen to us, it happens FOR us.

If someone has hurt you, let go and allow yourself to heal and grow from the experience.

You may even be able to get to a point where you learn to send love and appreciation to this person.
This is a simple ritual you can do every morning - write down a source of pain or resentment in your life, close your eyes, and allow yourself to let go and forgive.

Say out loud, "I forgive you."

Send love and compassion to them.

It may take time, depending on the pain, but you'll find that it'll begin to free you and more happiness can flow into your life.

Random Acts of Kindness

There is no better way to experience a sense of purpose and fulfillment in life than to contribute to the lives of others.

Here's a challenge for you: do one small thing every morning to contribute to someone else's life.

Send a text message, write a gratitude letter, or make a phone call to someone who has made a positive impact in your life.

You could also contribute to the lives' of strangers by giving $1 to a homeless person each day or giving love to random people online by commenting on their Facebook posts or YouTube videos, or tagging someone in an inspirational quote on Instagram.

A few words or a simple act of kindness could change someone's entire day.

People want to know that other people care about them.

The beauty of contribution is that it can have a ripple effect. If you can create moments and experiences like that and be a force for good by making a difference in the lives of others, do it.

Make a small difference in the world every day. Don't make your morning ritual to just be about YOU. The purpose of a ritual is to be able to grow and be your best in order to give to others.

In the words of Tony Robbins, *"It is not what we get, but who we become, and what we contribute, that gives meaning to our lives.*

Guided Meditation

In our fast paced, ever-changing world, meditation is becoming more important than ever before. The challenge that a lot of people have is committing to a practice that involves sitting in silence and clearing the mind, without any guidance.

This is why guided meditation is so helpful, in that it supports you, by way of spoken words, through the state of meditation.

You don't need to know *how* to meditate. All that matters is that you are present, listen, and allow the words to effortlessly move into your subconscious mind.

The purpose of a guided meditation is to help you come to a place of deep stillness, allowing your mind to declutter itself of negative thoughts and be replaced with high vibe images and positive visualizations.

There are a number of amazing effects, both cellular and hormonal, that come about through the process of guided meditation:

- Slows down brain wave activity and subdues stress all the while triggering human growth hormones (HGH).
- Helps calm the adrenals and allow them to rest, relieving them from over-producing cortisol, which is the stress hormone.
- Alkalizes your system, balancing out acidity that has accrued through the overactivity of your analytical mind and fear-based thinking.
- Decreases inflammation at the cellular level, neutralizing acidosis and minimizing pain.

Guided meditation has the power to heal and transform your life.

Spend some time every morning visualizing what it is that you want to manifest into your life.

When you train your brain to relax and slow down, you receive more clarity. This is one of the greatest gifts that you can give yourself.

Today, there's some incredible apps and devices that can help us optimize our meditation experience and make it more enjoyable.

My favorite is using the Muse, which helps to track your brainwaves while meditating and helps you get into a calm state: http://projectlifemastery.com/muse

Ho'oponopono Prayer

Ho'oponopono is an ancient Hawaiian practice of reconciliation and forgiveness.

If you are trying to heal or clear something in your life, saying this prayer out loud every morning is a powerful way to create more love, peace, and prosperity into your life.

In the 1980's Dr. Hew Len healed an entire ward of dangerous mentally ill criminals at the Hawaii State Hospital through the use of the Ho'oponopono Prayer.

Since then, healers and teachers have witnessed the spontaneous healing powers that have accompanied the act of forgiveness.

When faced with any adverse situation, a Ho'oponopono practitioner will immediately ask, *"What is it in me that is causing this event to take place, this person to behave this way, or this sickness to manifest?*' They believe that we are 100% responsible for everything in our lives.

Focus on healing YOURSELF. When you do, everything else will fall into place.

In the words of Ralph Smart, *"Words are powerful vibrations. Use them to uplift your spirits and heal yourself."*

A great book to learn more about Ho'oponopono is the book Zero Limits by Joe Vitale.

Prayer

The morning is a perfect time to set intentions and connect with your inner spirit, either through a daily prayer or a mantra.

Doing so will allow you to start your day with a sense of purpose, peace, and gratitude. Whatever your worldview is, sometimes a quick prayer can be all that you need to put yourself in an optimal state.

Scientists have proposed that prayer may be another means through which individuals protect themselves from breakdowns in one's will. One study suggested that priming individuals with words related to religion actually protected them against the effects of cognitive reduction.

Prayer is your *high speed* connection to something greater than yourself. Find what works best for you.

Someone once said, "*Faith is like WiFi, it has the power to connect you to what you need.*"

Heart Meditation

Whereas traditional meditation focuses on calming the mind, a heart meditation is more feeling-centered. It is your opportunity to connect to your inner Source of light and love.

The idea behind a heart meditation is that everything that you've ever wanted already resides within you.

When we are looking for answers to life's greatest questions, we need to tune into our body and listen to our intuitive center - our heart. This is a place that never lies. It is the seat of our Truth.

A heart meditation allows you to gently release any emotions that are preventing you from living your best self. It helps us forgive ourselves and others so that we can find freedom from guilt and resentment, and in turn, live a more loving and heart-centered existence.

When you are more deeply connected to your heart, it will allow for more abundance to come into your life because you will be more in alignment with your true Self.

Spend the morning tuning into your heart space and honor what it needs. When you do so, your actions will flow with greater ease and clarity.

In the words of Mingtong Gu, *"Open your heart, ignite the flame in your being, and awaken the natural flow of life energy in your heart. When your heart opens, the world around you changes."*

A great book to learn more about heart-centred meditation is The HeartMath Solution: The Institute Of HeartMath's Revolutionary Program For Engaging The Power Of The Heart's Intelligence.

They have a great device and app that I use in conjunction with the Muse, called Inner Balance:
http://projectlifemastery.com/innerbalance

Celebrate You

Start your mornings by acknowledging every action that you have taken towards the achievement of your goals. It is so important to celebrate you.

Oftentimes, we don't give ourselves enough credit for our accomplishments. The more that you do so, the more success you will have.

You may be wondering, *"But what if I didn't do anything special this week?"*

Every little effort that you make towards your personal growth and development deserves to be celebrated. The more that you acknowledge and reward yourself for all of your successes, the more success you will have.

You may be wondering, *"How is this possible?"*

The neurons associated with a certain activity function together and form a neural pathway. By continually celebrating you, the connections between these neural pathways become established and stronger.

Stanford University professor and habit expert, B.J. Fogg first popularized the celebrations concept which states that celebrating immediately after completing a healthy habit creates a memory imprint in your mind.

Make an effort to integrate celebration into each part of your morning ritual. If you don't celebrate you, nobody will.

Self-Love

The relationship that you have with yourself is one of the most important relationships that you will ever have. So many of us freely give our love to others, but what about us?

Research suggests that self-acceptance leads to greater satisfaction with your life, but it's a habit that many people practice the least.

More than just a state of feeling good about yourself, self-love is an action. There is no better way to start your day than by nourishing and showing kindness to yourself.

However, in order to make self-love 'stick', you need to commit to practicing it every day.

When we love ourselves more, we have more fulfilling relationships with others, feel more grounded in our life's purpose, and make choices that are aligned with our highest self. Self-love is the greatest love of all.

A simple way you can do this is to look yourself in the mirror each morning, deep in the eyes and say, "I love you."

To go even deeper, tell yourself all of the things that you love about yourself and compliment yourself on everything.

Taking care of yourself isn't selfish. Rather, it's a priority.

Put yourself at the top of your to-do list every day. When you do, everything else will fall into place.

In the words of Robert Morley, *"To fall in love with yourself is the first secret to happiness."*

Recite A Mantra

Starting your day with a mindful morning mantra is a great way to make you feel more present, grateful, and grounded.

A mantra is a word or sound that is meant to be chanted aloud or repeated silently.

Oftentimes, our minds are consumed with a lot of negative self-talk but the good news is that you have the power to create your reality with your thoughts.

Reading a mantra out loud is like doing a mini-meditation for your brain.

When you feed your mind with positive thoughts, you attract positive things into your life which increases your chances of success and makes life sweeter.

Mantra repetition has been found to initiate profound changes in the physiological systems of the body, some of which include enhancing alpha brain wave activity, and lowering stress hormone levels.

A popular Sanskrit mantra is the word, OM, which is said to represent the sound of the Universe. This is a great mantra to use at the beginning or end of a yoga class, or if you are seeking stillness.

If you commit to bringing mantras into your daily morning routine, you will begin to see a shift in your mindset and your entire day.

Set An Intention For The Day

Everything in life starts with an intention, from waking up, to making breakfast, to going for a run.

Setting an intention for the day is about taking the time to acknowledge your feelings.

When you are clear about how you want to feel, it allows you to make decisions that are in alignment with your authentic self.

Intentions reflect the power of our consciousness to create our version of reality. When we are clear about what we really want in life and focus on it every day, we can manifest it.

The power of intentions is best reflected in the water molecule experiments of Dr. Masaru Emoto, who demonstrated that human thoughts and intentions can alter physical reality.

The classic Vedic text,, known as the *Upanishads* declares, *"You are what your deepest desire is. As your desire is, so is your intention. As your intention is, so is your will. As your will is, so is your deed. As your deed is, so is your destiny."*

Just because you set an intention, that doesn't mean that it will magically appear. It requires commitment, persistence, and a deep desire to work towards whatever it is that you desire most.

Write A Love Letter To Yourself

It may sound cheesy but writing a love letter to yourself is one of the greatest gifts that you can give yourself. It is a beautiful reminder that self-love is the best kind of love.

Many of us are really hard on ourselves and tend to put ourselves down when we make mistakes of any kind. These are the moments when we need to show ourselves the most love.

A growing body of research shows that people who respond to mistakes with self-compassion rather than self-criticism maintain healthier emotional equilibrium and manage challenges better than those who don't.

Now and again we all need to be reminded how amazing, talented, and courageous we are, and who better to do it than you?

Imagine that you are writing a letter to your best friend. What would you say?

A self-love letter to oneself is the purest form of self-acceptance.

This isn't an egotistical exercise. Rather, it is your opportunity to speak to your inner self and show gratitude for the person that you are and how far you've come.

In her book, "Self-Compassion", pioneer researcher Kristin Neuff suggests that self-compassion means treating yourself as you would a friend, in times of failure and pain, with more understanding and kindness.

Every morning, take out your self-love letter and read it to yourself, reminding yourself how amazing you are.

In the words of Brene Brown, *"Talk to yourself like you would to someone you love."* Once you start appreciating you for you, others will start doing the same.

Record Your Dreams

Have you ever woken up from a dream and felt as if it were real?

Your dreams are telling you more than you may think.

Sigmund Freud once said that, "The interpretation of dreams is the royal road to a knowledge of the unconscious activities of the mind."

The problem that a lot of people face is that they wake up from a dream not remembering what happened.

This is why I'm a big believer in writing down my dreams first thing in the morning.

Not only is it a great way to understand yourself on a deeper level, but it can also be an extremely therapeutic process. It's a way of telling your unconscious mind that you are receptive to listening to it.

Research shows that REM-sleep dreaming appears to take the painful sting out of difficult, even traumatic, emotional episodes experienced during the day.

In a sense, dreaming is like therapy for your restless mind. Dreams really are a window into your soul.

Make it a habit of recording your dreams every morning so that you don't forget them!

Over time, you will start to notice connections between your dreams and your current emotional state, which will help to deepen your understanding of your inner world.

Practice Your Spirituality

Spirituality is a state of mind, something that brings you more connected to your higher self and true purpose in life.

What practice do you engage in that allows you to find your center, so that you can move throughout your day feeling guided by inner love and peace?

A great way to grow spiritually is to read text that instills your faith in a power that is greater than yourself.

Dr. Steven Southwick's book, "Resilience: The Science of Mastering Life's Greatest Challenges", describes that having a strong spiritual outlook may help you find meaning in life's difficult circumstances. The practice of acknowledging the interconnectedness of all forms of life can help shield against the pain that comes with adversity and hardship.

Spirituality has also been found to be good for your health and wellbeing.

Research shows that people who practice religion or a faith tradition are less likely to drink or smoke or commit a crime, and are more likely to engage in preventative habits.

Keep in mind that a spiritual practice doesn't mean that you have to ascribe to a specific religion. It can be in the form of reading the bible, poetry, an excerpt from a book of meditations, prayer, or a psalm. Any practice that directs your attention inward, restores your faith and hope, and increases compassion for yourself and others, is good for you.

Read Spiritual Text

A great way to build your spiritual muscle is by making it a habit of reading something spiritually uplifting every single day.

This could be in the form of a quote or scripture.

By connecting and having an intentional conversation with Source, in whatever form that means for you, it will help to elevate your vibration.

When you are in this empowering state of mind, you will be better able to move into your day feeling grounded.

Reading spiritual messages will give meaning to your life and put you directly into a state of unconditional love and gratitude.

Despite whatever you may be going through in life, allow your spiritual messages to guide you into a better tomorrow. Never give up faith on what could be.

In the words of Corrie ten Boom, "Faith sees the invisible, believes the unbelievable and receives the impossible."

NEXT STEPS

Hopefully by now you're excited, and your brain is buzzing with ideas for your new empowering morning ritual.

I've been doing morning rituals since I was 17 years old, and it's without a doubt one of the most powerful tools for radically transforming your entire life.

Would you like my help in creating your ideal empowering morning ritual?

A morning ritual that will take your body, mind, spirit, relationships, career, business and finances to the next level?

If so, I want to invite you to join my Morning Ritual Mastery program.

Inside I share how you can model the most successful morning rituals of the happiest and successful people on the planet, so that you can create a morning ritual that produces RESULTS.

Morning Ritual Mastery is a 7-day program that will guide you step-by-step through the process of creating and implementing a morning ritual that is customized to your personal goals, dreams and desires.

By the end of the 7 days you will have an empowering morning ritual that will be a permanent part of your life, and that will produce the results and quality of life you desire.

To learn more, go to: www.morningritualmastery.com

I should also mention that there is a full 100% money back guarantee, so there's absolutely no risk on your part.

So give it a try.

I promise you, you will not regret it!

Wishing you a lifetime of empowered mornings,

Stefan James

Founder of Project Life Mastery
www.projectlifemastery.com

54623118R00054

Made in the USA
Columbia, SC
03 April 2019